REACHING YOUR VETERINARY CAREER SUCCESS

Dr Vadim Chelom

© Vadim Chelom 2017

Dear Reader. I hope you enjoy this book and find it useful. Please refrain from distributing or copying this book in any form without my permission.

This book is dedicated to my family and the families of Veterinarians everywhere. Without them we couldn't be who we are.

Contents

Why you need to read this book	5
Understanding your professional value	17
Demonstrating professional value	34
Why your boss is paying you as much as he does and what you can do about it	49
How to negotiate a spectacular pay rise	70
The importance of definitive diagnosis	79
A word about in-house laboratory testing	92
How to perform a routine vaccination	103
How to resolve customer complaints	123
The basics of veterinary marketing	133
Managing your time	153
Maintaining your emotional health	171
The chapter with nothing after it yet	195

Why You Need To Read This Book

I was standing at a bus stop in the bright autumn sun just outside Tel-Aviv pondering my difficult situation. Things were getting desperate. An outsider in a foreign country, with little language and without a support network, I was badly in need of a steady income. I had 13 years' experience as a Veterinarian in Australia working in private practice, the animal welfare sector and in an emergency hospital. My clinical skills were solid and I thought I could work anywhere. The job I got - at a Jerusalem SPCA, did provide some income. I also learned to perform routine surgeries faster and more efficiently then I have ever imagined. But the hours were limited and irregular. What I needed to give my family a steady income was a regular full time wage. So when an offer came to work for an education company for a customer service role, I said Yes right away.

The position I signed up for was for Customer Retention in a large international company providing online language education. It sounded reasonable enough on paper. Little did I know what I was getting into. In any business there are disgruntled customers, who have, rightly or wrongly decided that this company is not for them. They may be unhappy about the price, quality of service, lack of attention, how they were spoken to by the receptionist, whatever. They have tried and failed to resolve their problem via regular customer service channels and have decided to quit the company altogether. They are now leaving, upset, one foot out the door. Guess who gets to speak to them now - Customer Retention. I should have wondered why there were so few applicants for this position! No matter - the money was good and they were flexible about previous experience (I don't think my soft tissue surgery skills is what sold me as a candidate). So back to the disgruntled customer - picture your worst disgruntled client multiplied by ten. This is where I come in. My job is to bring them back into the fold and convince them to give their language course another go.

It goes without saying that all my customers - every one of them, were angry, upset, demanding recourse and generally not in a good conversational mood. The only way I could succeed is learn on the job and do it quick. I learned to deflect the initial criticism and abuse, I learned to keep them talking for long enough to give me the keys to develop a solution and that the real problem is usually not the problem described in words.

Of course as part of my special role I had a set of special tools. My customers had one foot out the door, so the company was prepared to pull out all stops to help them change their mind. I could change their class schedules, assign them new teachers, give additional lessons and - the holy grail of them all - offer generous fee discounts. These were great but they didn't make or break the outcome. I learned quickly that what the customers wanted was a solution. The solution had to address the real problem. It needed to come with an action plan, a timeline and measurable goals.

Sometimes I would win outright and the customer would be thankful for my efforts.

Those times were very rare. Overtime I learned to take the 'Ok, I will think about it' reply as a sign of a victory - winning the first round with the next round to follow. Slowly I became better at the job. This was good because my paycheck was linked to how many customers I can retain, so the more I retained the more I got paid.

I didn't think the Customer Retention job would do any good to my Veterinary career. In fact I thought of it as an annoying detour from the work I actually wanted to do. I learned how wrong I was about that when one year later I returned to Australia and started working as a Veterinarian again. I didn't think I was doing anything different but everyone else thought that my customer service skills were in a different class. Most people hate dealing with disgruntled customers. They try to push that dreaded task off to the end of the day, or preferably into somebody else's in-tray. I don't love dealing with complaints either - a complaint means that someone in the team probably messed up. But I relish the challenge the way a noble Samurai relishes the opportunity to battle an equally noble opponent, for the same reason JF Kennedy committed America to put a man on the moon (I could keep going with irrelevant analogies but you get the idea). Because nothing beats the feeling of turning a complaint all the way around - into a loyal customer. I also learned to think backwards and identify situations which are more likely to lead to a complaint arising (Situations - not mistakes. Looking backwards everyone can spot a mistake). Unlike what most of us think, Veterinarians usually fail not due to lack of professional knowledge but failures of communication. In fact, lack of knowledge need not be an impediment at all - we can't know everything. Admitting our limitations can be a sign of professional maturity and can actually increase trust and customer satisfaction - if we communicate it correctly.

As a manager of seven Veterinarians and two clinics, I find it astonishing that what makes my work a success was never taught to me during my university studies. I was taught to look for a diagnosis, not for a solution. A diagnosis is a very important component of finding a solution, but it's only one component. Where my Veterinary training was most glaringly inadequate was in my (lack of) customer communication. So when I decided to write down the things in my career that worked, the first chapter I wrote was about resolving customer complaints.

I then added chapters about Veterinary marketing, financial management, emotional health - the more I thought about (holes in) my University education, the more subject areas came to light. I could have called this book 'All the things my Veterinary degree didn't teach me but I wish it did', which would be too long and also slightly disrespectful to my University professors, whom I admire greatly (even though their wages are higher than mine and their work day is much shorter).

If you are a new or recent Veterinary graduate, you should make reading this book a top priority. It will help you develop you commutation skills in ways and areas that your Degree has never taught you. Don't just stop at reading this book - take every available opportunity to develop your customer service skills. You should prioritise it higher than say, developing the skills of orthopaedic surgery. After all, you can usually refer orthopaedic surgery, but you can't refer an angry client to go and complain to another clinic down the road.

But perhaps you are not a new graduate at all, but an experienced Veterinary professional like myself. Perhaps you have, through the twists and turns of your own life journey, developed a finely tuned set of customer service tools of your own. If so, chances are that in this area of practice you are entirely self-taught, just like the rest of us. Your methods may be just as good or better than mine, but I'll bet a dollar that your methods are entirely different. I anticipate that you will enjoy learning another way - delving into the head of someone in similar shoes but with a different box of tricks up his sleeve. You may even find some new ideas to use for yourself. Or maybe one day it will inspire you to write a help book of your own. I for one wish it would, because if so, you can count me as your first loyal reader.

Understanding Your Professional Value

OK, I know you are about to call me a liar. Just before I said that the first chapter written by me was the 'Solving Customer Complaints' chapter. And yet this is clearly not that chapter. Why did I change the order? Because without reading and understanding this section first, you can't solve any customer complaints. None. Zero. You can't even get out of bed in the morning. Actually, yes you can, but you can't open the door and call the first client into your consulting room. Because everything you do in your work day, everything you are going to charge money for is predicated upon you understanding clearly the professional value and the business proposition of that little Veterinary problem-solving centre - namely You.

It is accepted wisdom that Veterinarians struggle to properly charge for their services. It is also well known that the general public sees Veterinary care as unreasonably expensive. Researchers, statisticians and others with nothing much to do with their day, make many suggestions to explain this - from the cheaper appearance of the government subsidised human medical care, to the relatively low purchase cost of pets compared to their health care 'running' costs. These arguments however fail to explain how other professions, such as lawyers and accountants are able to command much higher per hour fees for their (arguably less skilled) services and have instilled an unshakable belief in the general population, that paying $500 for a one page lawyer's letter is entirely fair and reasonable.

The reason clearly lies not with the unique qualities of our work but with our ability as a profession to communicate the Value of our work. This brings us to the critical topic of your Professional Value.

What is your Professional Value and is it important to know it? Is knowing your professional value more important than knowing say, the normal PCV range for a dog or the indications for chemotherapy in a cat with a soft tissue sarcoma? The answer is, like a shining light glowing brightly in the sky and eliminating every step you take in your day and in your career, your Professional Value underpins all your professional decision making. It's what gives you the confidence to open the consulting room door in the morning to call your first patient in. It's what motivates you to recommend the diagnostic and treatment steps you feel are appropriate in the cases that you see. If you don't know it and you don't value it, you can't possibly communicate it to anyone.

So what is your Professional Value?

You may be a highly qualified and experienced specialist in your field able to provide the most up to date diagnostic and treatment options. This knowledge and skills will help you greatly in your work but it doesn't reflect your Professional Value.

You may have committed years of your life to the unpaid task of your Veterinary training. In addition to that you may be carrying a sizable student debt which needs paying off, as well as other financial commitments, such as mortgage payments and family expenses. These are important considerations but they in no way define your Professional Value.

The way I like to think about it is like this:

Your Professional Value is the monetary value your client puts on your ability to solve their problems.

As you see from this definition, your Professional Value is not defined by you. It is the client who at the end of the consultation takes out her wallet and pays your fees. So does that mean that the way you are valued is out of your reach? No, of course it doesn't. In fact, it is entirely in your hands. You can't make the client value your work but you can control many of the factors which determine whether or not the client will do so.

This represents a radical departure from the traditional diagnosis/treatment paradigm taught to the Veterinary students everywhere. A Veterinary graduate is taught to see themselves as a little diagnosis and treatment machine, and once he/she has found the right diagnosis and prescribed an appropriate treatment for it, this is seen as the pinnacle of Veterinary profession and all it is capable of.

I am now asking you to close your eyes, take a deep breath and let go of the ludicrous notion that diagnosis and treatment are all you are capable off. That's not so say that diagnosis and treatment are not important, on the contrary - they lie at the core of the complex and valuable service we provide. What I am telling you is that this is precisely the part of the service our clients do not see and cannot meaningfully measure the true value of.

Take the services of a specialist surgeon for example. She may spend hours performing an intricate and complex orthopaedic or soft tissue procedure, but all the client will see at the end is a neat row of sutures. The client will never know which method was chosen to perform the procedure, how careful her haemostasis technique was or which suture pattern was chosen for the wound closure. The client will see what the wound looks like - how neatly the hair was clipped and if there is any blood around the wound, how nice the waiting room looks and whether the reception staff is friendly and helpful.

The client will probably evaluate the surgeon's performance based on those subjective factors, regardless of how irrelevant they may be to the surgeon's actual professional ability.

As Veterinarians, we must understand that how we do things, or more precisely how we are *seen* to be doing things in arriving to the conclusion of each case, will impact on the way we are judged by our clients every bit as much as the conclusion itself. In the pages to come, I will be explaining a great deal about which steps and techniques can help you to improve the way this silent communication is carried out. I hope you will find some of them helpful, or at least use them as food for thought to develop your own. But even before you start reading the details, consider pausing for a moment and acknowledging in your mind that the way you interact with the client - the way you walk and talk and how you use your hands and what mannerisms you use, impacts greatly on your clients' recognition and appreciation of your work. This recognition in itself greatly impacts on the way you do your work every day.

As scientists, we are taught to reject the subjective factors. We are taught that only evidence matters and that feelings and emotions are inconvenient distractions to be ignored on the way to finding the truth. But our clients live in the world filled with feelings and emotions, especially when it comes to their pets. They want our emotions to be the mirror of theirs. They will judge an unemotional Veterinarian to be not objective, but cold and uncaring. On the other hand, you can not allow yourself to become submerged in your clients' feelings. If you do, it will gradually drain your own emotional reserves, leaving you exhausted and burned out at the end of every working day.

As Veterinarians, we must learn to control how much of our clients' feelings we are prepared to absorb. This is cold and calculated, but a necessary professional skill, which allows us to provide our clients comfort and support that they need without causing us, Veterinary professionals, long term emotional harm.

We must also learn to project confidence and conviction, even as we navigate the medical world full of diagnostic uncertainty. Remember - *communicating uncertainty is not the same as feeling uncertainty.* I feel perfectly confident communicating the uncertainties of the treatment options for a particular neoplasia, for example, while feeling unwavering certainty in the strength of my advice.

The first step to communicating it is feeling it within yourself. If you feel doubtful about your decisions and recommendations, this doubt will seep into everything you do - the way you talk, the way you hold yourself, etc. You will struggle to persuade your client in the value of your service if you yourself don't believe in that value.

Self-confidence is a personality trait. Some of us have lots of it, others not so much. If you are a naturally confident person and always speak your mind clearly and with conviction, it will make it easier for you to impress your Professional Value upon your clients. It will also probably help you impress your friends at dinner parties and when going out on dates. If you are that popular, confident person, then we all probably hate you but secretly wish we were more like you, and you probably don't care because you already have the persons of the opposite gender eating out of the palm of your hand. That's good for you but it doesn't help the rest of us.

The good news is, confidence is not innate. It is a skill everyone can improve in. You will feel more confident if you are dressed in smart, professional attire. You will feel more confident if you feel you have strong peer-reviewed evidence for the things you are saying. It's like having an invisible gathering of professionals in white coats standing beside you as you speak, so make sure you have enough diagnostic evidence behind your back before you offer treatment solutions.

Just remember - the higher your professional value is in your own mind, the higher you can raise it in the minds of your clients. Think of it like this - on the stone at the entrance of many old courthouses in the US are engraved the Ten Commandments. They are not directly relevant to any of the cases heard in the courthouse. The Judge does not run outside to check their wording before issuing a verdict. And yet they define and inform (used to define and inform?) the very essence of what happens behind the court's doors.

Like the Ten Commandments in the Courthouse, so too is your sense and recognition of your Professional Value. It will not make your microscope slides clearer or help you aim your biopsy needle any better. But it will give every one of your professional decisions - in front of the client or behind closed doors, greater clarity and confidence.

So far we have talked about internal changes you can make within yourself. Now, we are about to discuss physical, tangible steps you can take to demonstrate this Value to your clients.

Demonstrating Professional Value

A Veterinarian calls a client in for a scheduled vaccination appointment. He then proceeds to perform a comprehensive clinical examination on the client's dog at the end of which, satisfied that the dog is in great state of health, the Veterinarian performs the necessary injections and bids the client goodbye. There is no doubt that analysing the health data he gained during the clinical examination, the Veterinarian used his extensive professional knowledge which he painstakingly collected during his grueling University studies and then further refined with years of experience. It is clear to you and I that this Veterinarian's final health assessment is of great value to the client and the patient. But the client is very likely not to see it that way. The client can not interpret the steps in the clinical examination as anything more than strange touching and feeling. What the client can see and understand is the part where the Veterinarian has taken out a syringe and gave the injection. This is exactly what he came for and what he is paying the Veterinarian to do. But what about the tremendous extra value contained within the clinical examination! The Veterinarian has just missed out on an opportunity to communicate so much more. She has failed to demonstrate the unique and special benefits of the intricate diagnostic procedure, which she just performed in front of the client's very nose. You would never imagine taking Fluffy out the back during a consultation to perform a quick little diagnostic ultrasound, without telling a word to the owner. Yet when it comes to a clinical exam, that is exactly what we do when we perform it while keeping our mouth shut. The Veterinarian has made no effort to create a perception of Value and on future occasions the client is no more likely to choose this Veterinarian than any other. He will probably choose to go to a clinic down the road if a cheaper alternative is presented to him, as no differentiating Value was presented to him other than the price.

I was once discussing with a client a tape prep procedure performed by another Veterinarian. The client evidently felt that the cost of the procedure was too expensive.

'He even used a Scotch tape.' The client explained frustrated.

'He could have use any supermarket tape but he used a Scotch tape.'

It struck me then how the client's perception of the Veterinarian's actions differed so greatly from the reality.

The Veterinarian would have collected the tape cytology sample in the consult room and then walked to the in-house laboratory to do the staining and microscope examination. He would have used his extensive cytology skills to stain, examine and interpret the data. Every one of those steps is a highly specialised skill for which professional clinical pathologists - animal and human, charge high fees. However the client saw none of these steps. All he saw and understood is the Scotch tape. If the Scotch tape represents the Value of the test, no wonder the client feels the test is overpriced and a cheaper alternative would suffice. Doesn't it pay sometimes to look at the situation from the client's point of view!

The week after that client conversation I moved my clinic lab into the room adjacent to the consultation room. This way when I left to perform an in-house test, the client could watch all of my actions through a glass window. After all, what gave this test its Value is not the slide or the microscope or the staining solution. It's the Veterinarian's skill, and by demonstrating the application of my skill I was giving the client a concrete understanding of what his money was paying for. In this way I was able to communicate Value and it cost me no extra time or effort to do it.

Veterinarians are often afraid to expose their 'back of house' activities to the public view. We all dislike being watched in our private moments, especially as we struggle sometimes to organise our thoughts. For me it was a learning curve to get used to do my cytology work while being watched like a goldfish in a tank.

No one likes being judged. What we often forget is that the clients are not judging us - they are admiring us. Most clients are fascinated by what we do and absolutely love catching every glimpse of our work. This fascination doesn't diminish if they see us stumble or look unsure of ourselves, maybe even the opposite. After all, isn't that why all those Veterinary reality shows are so popular. By letting the client into your world you are actually creating a very powerful bond that will last long after the appointment is finished, and a value proposition which sets you apart from others.

The general rule should be: the more communication - verbal and nonverbal, the better. To be sure, there are procedures that you would want to do away from the client: anything which may make their pet appear distressed (even when you know that the procedure is safe for the pet and necessary for their health), anything involving blood etc. But this list is much shorter than most Veterinarians think.

I don't just perform my in-house cytology in view of the client, I also invite them to look through the microscope if they wish. Most say No, some say Yes. In either case, the client feels the level of participation and insight which goes beyond their regular Veterinary experience (and you will be surprised how many of you clients have laboratory background and will give you staining and interpretation advice). One of my clients I discovered is a human laboratory technician, so whenever I need a sample of her chronic UTI cat's urine cytology, she does the preparation for me. I still charge her the regular fee but she does all the work - and she loves it.

With this participation mantra in mind I preserve the patient's extracted teeth and soft tissue masses after a procedure for a client to view if they wish. Following similar approach, a Veterinary colleague uses an iPad to record small videos of each surgery and invites the client to watch afterwards. The videos are only a few minutes long and are heavily redacted to avoid showing anything confronting or distressing, but it's enough to create a feeling of 'being there'. Not every client would want to see the removed teeth or watch the video, but all will appreciate the added insight.

Another very important skill is verbally communicating your thoughts and findings to the client. Normal findings are just as important insight as abnormal findings. We all start gathering our medical database pretty much from the moment we open the door and call the client in. We watch the way the animal walks, how it postures, is it anxious or relaxed. Often I would be starting the data gathering process before I actually see the patient. As I sit in my consulting room completing previous patient's history, I hear the loud breathing, listen to the coughing or the tembre of the bark. This is highly valuable information gathered for the patient's benefit. And the client has no idea!

Let's say, I am palpating the popliteal lymph nodes or checking the femoral pulse. Naturally the client will not understand what I am doing. All she sees is me touching the dog in weird ways. So how should I use this as an educational opportunity to demonstrate the Value of my service? I should verbally communicate the meaning of my actions and what my findings are! Would you imagine a Lawyer going over his client's brief just to kill time or an Accountant filling out tax returns out of curiosity? No you would not. Because these highly skilled professionals make an effort to communicate the Value of their skill to the client at all times. And so should you.

What this means in practice is me giving a kind of live verbal narration of my actions. As I am progressing through the clinical examination, I am describing what I am doing and what my findings are. I may say that the puppy I am examining has good bite, healthy teeth strong femoral pulse, normal eye responses and so on. It doesn't need to be complicated or worded in an overly scientific language. Just a brief summary of what I am doing at any particular moment in time.

In this context indicating normal findings is just as important as the abnormal ones. People love hearing out loud all the things which are going well with their pet. You can say that he has great bite, nice posture, shiny coat, etc. If you tell Mrs Smith that Fluffy has healthy teeth, she will be ecstatic. She will probably go to the dog park and tell everyone how good Fluffy's teeth are and how nice that Vet is who told her so. It doesn't matter that at eight months old, there are very few things which could be going wrong with

Fluffy's teeth. You know that but Mrs Smith doesn't. She is just happy that Fluffy is healthy. And next time she comes back for the scheduled revisit, she would be waiting to hear about the progress of Fluffy's teeth. So that when an actual problem is detected, she will be ready to fix it right away.

On the other hand, an owner I once saw was very surprised when I explained to her that her dog may be soon requiring a dental procedure. She was previously seen at another clinic and was never told about the plaque and tartar gradually building up on her dog's teeth. Now suddenly she was told that there is a problem that needed a medical procedure. The failure of the previous Veterinarian to provide this information made the owner angry and upset. She felt that she was kept in the dark about her pet's state of health. And that her not knowing about the problem may have caused her pet pain and discomfort. Always make sure you paint as full a picture of your patients' health as possible, including what may appear to you as trivial details. Your clients will thank you for it.

Why Your Boss Is Paying You As Much As He Does and What You Can Do About It

Do Veterinary wages reflect the level of training and skill required to practice within our profession? Whoa, just take it easy now! Sit back in your chair and stop shouting. People are staring at you.

We all know just how contentious the issue of Veterinary pay has been over the years. If I say that Veterinarians, saddled with heavy University debt and out of the workforce for extensive periods of time due to their studies, are significantly underpaid relative to other comparable professions, I would be stating the obvious and probably opening a raw wound.

But it is one thing to complain and quite another to try to analyse the situation in the hope of finding a solution. In the employment marketplace Veterinarians are entrepreneurs competing against each other for the limited number of jobs on offer. In this competitive environment they may be assisted by their knowledge of the job market, their level of experience, specialisation or the ability to 'sell themselves'. The impending Veterinary oversupply driven by large numbers of graduates being produced by the major Universities, is another significant factor often talked about within the profession.

'Blah, blah, blah' you say 'Nothing I haven't heard before here'. Fair point, but just keep reading, it's about to get better.

Complaining is all good and well, but without basic understanding of Veterinary clinic economics talking about employment is like attending a Homeopathy class - meaningless mumbo-jumbo and a complete waste of your time.

So to make this a more realistic experience, I am about to transport you to a virtual Veterinary clinic playroom, where everything is possible, unicorns frolic in the meadows and more importantly, we can work through some hypothetical Veterinary financial scenarios.

Please note, the dollar numbers below are not based on any real example but are composites of the typical clinic scenarios I have experienced over the years. The numbers are also rounded off (brutally) to make them easier to work with, so please don't write in complaining that the values don't add up to the nearest 5 dollars.

So let's begin. I am now transplanting you into your Virtual Clinic. It is a small clinic where you are the only Veterinarian on duty. This clinic is open 9am to 7pm - 10 business hours with no after hours. On this particular day you are having a reasonably quiet time at the office with nothing terribly exciting to interrupt your day. You have booked in six appointments and three surgeries - all routine and straightforward.

Your consultation appointments have paid on average $100 each and your three surgeries (you know, routine things like a desexing, an abscesses and maybe a dental procedure) have paid $400 each. While you were busy doing those, your reception nurse has managed to sell $200 worth of pet food and preventatives over the counter.

So all together, on this quiet unassuming day your Virtual Clinic has managed to earn a cool $2000. Not a bad day at the office, easy money earned without breaking a sweat.

Now before you march into your boss's office and ask for a $1000 a day pay rise, let's look at the bigger picture, namely how much earning those $2000 cost your boss.

First of all - the fixed costs. That's the cash which got paid up before you opened the door. You know - rent, rates, operating licenses and all that. In our case we will count this day's rent at $200 (a reasonable 10% of the earnings). The rest of that day's fixed costs we will lump together into a neat $100, just to make the maths easier.

And don't forget depreciation - that's the money your boss is paying to the bank for all those expensive diagnostic toys and equipment you get to play with. Let's round that off to another neat $100.

Now let's count Cost of Goods Sold. That's how much your day's sold items and used up consumables actually cost the clinic to buy. We all know that many clinics will mark up medications by 100%. Food and general pet care items are marked up much less - sometimes as little as 10-20% to make the prices more in line with pet shops and online stores. With surgical procedures, add the cost of the consumable items you used - catheters, medications, etc. Probably 30-40% of the cost of the procedure. Let's say our Cost of Goods sold is $600 for the day. That's 30% of earnings - again a very reasonable number in a real life scenario.

So now our $2000 earnings have been trimmed down to $1000 (2000-600-200-100-100 =1000).

That's still a nice bit of money to make for a day's work. But wait, we are forgetting the very important expense line. The most important expense line actually. The one that probably keeps your boss up at night. I am of course talking about wages.

First of all there is you, the Vet. In our Virtual Clinic you are employed on a full time rate of $40/h. Therefore on this particular day you are walking away with $380 ($40x9.5 hours excluding 30 minute lunch break). This is a little less than how much your boss is actually paying for you, because you also need your entitlement hours (annual leave, sick leave, study leave) covered, probably by locums. So to accommodate those costs we will add a 20% premium which will bring your daily cost to approximately $450 ($456 actually, but who is counting).

Then there is the Nurses' wage. We all know how low Veterinary Nurse wages are, and your Virtual Clinic is pretty typical, paying at $20/hour. As many clinics do, our Clinic is staffed by two Nurses overlapping in the middle of the day to allow for lunchtime coverage and a dedicated assistant to help with surgery. We will allocate $300 for the day's

Nursing wages to cover 1.5 Nurses for 10 hours.

Now our expenses list is almost complete. Let's not forget the taxes, on which we will allocate $50.

Now to add up the numbers - the wages and taxes have cost us $800(450+300+50). Once we add this to our fixed and variable costs of $1000, We are left with a paltry profit of $200, which at 10% of earnings is a not uncommon number in the industry, and this is how much your boss will actually take home (after he pays his personal income tax from it). Which is a whole lot less than the amount you are taking home (granted that you have spent the whole day working, while your boss was probably on the golf course practicing his swing).

This is quite an enlightening exercise, and it paints the Veterinary industry and the role you play in it in very different light. As a new graduate, such business-like dollars-and-cents approach was completely foreign to me. I simply did not understand (did not *care* to understand) the Veterinary business model. I only acquired this view when I as a manager became responsible for looking at my clinic's monthly Profit and Loss statements and reporting on them to my own Managers. Which is a shame, because if someone during my University days or soon after has bothered to sit me down and explain the bare basics of Veterinary business, this would have enormously expanded my understanding of how my routine Veterinary decisions impact on the Veterinary business operation. This is the kind of knowledge which separates a rank and file Veterinarian from 'management material'.

In view of this, allow me to make some blatantly obvious and yet strikingly important observations:

- Veterinary business is high turnover business. A lot of money comes in, a lot of money goes out. The costs -

both fixed and variable, of running a Veterinary clinic are astronomically high compared to many other service industries. A lawyer or an accountant sits in an office having to outlay rent and maybe Wi-Fi cost (unless he is stealing Wi-Fi from the office next door), while charging per-hour fees comparable to the surgery-time fees of an orthopaedic specialist Veterinarian, who is probably paying three support staff and a significant leasing fee for his fancy capital equipment. The (perceived) high costs of Veterinary care are a reflexion of high expense of providing such care. The after-tax profits of Veterinary clinics are frequently in the vicinity of a few percent of turnover.

- Your boss's biggest expense item is not that shiny new piece of diagnostic equipment she recently purchased. Your boss's biggest expense item is you. Yes, You, even if you feel that you are the lowest paid sucker of all your high school friends (even the ones who went to TAFE). It is well known that in the Veterinary industry wages routinely eat up 50-60% of the earnings. Combine this with the fact that an employee investment is the ultimate long term investment (your boss can easily retire or sell-on a non performing piece of equipment, moving-on a non performing employee can be a very difficult proposition). You can now clearly see that you are your boss's biggest expense item and a huge liability.

- If you look again at our calculations, you will notice that different types of services contribute to the clinic's bottom line in very different ways. Consumable items, such as pet food and preventables, are generally sold at very low margin, because the clinic is competing with other pet retail channels, such as pet shops and online stores. For most clinics, product sales are a healthy and important source of additional income, but they do not significantly impact on the success of the clinic's core business. The same applies to dispensing medications. A veterinary clinic's core business is providing veterinary care. That is us - Veterinarians like you and I, using our skills in diagnostics, medicine and surgery to provide solutions for our valued clients, and to charge for them appropriately.

- I have just made this point in the line above, but I am going to make it again because a profound piece of Veterinary wisdom like this deserves a dedicated bullet point of its' own. In fact I might emphasise it further by writing it in bold. **We the highly professional Veterinarians, contribute to the success of our employment not by mindlessly dispensing medications (who hasn't on occasion dispensed a combination of antibiotics and prednisolone without having a faintest idea about what they are treating, but that's another story), but by engaging our highly trained Veterinary minds to precisely pinpoint and resolve the problem.** In other words, **a healthy Veterinary clinic has a**

healthy flow of in-house laboratory work and surgical procedures. When evaluating the performance of a clinic or an individual Veterinarian, this metric - expressed as a percentage of appointment numbers, is the first parameter I look at.

- What makes this earth-shattering revelation even more exciting, is that the same features which create a financially healthy and productive Veterinary clinic, also serve to foster happy and satisfied Veterinary clients. This is a truly unique combination rarely found in business elsewhere. Unlike most of the rest of the business world, which sells pre-made rigid products to the customer, our industry is in the business of selling solutions. Each solution is as unique as each of our patients, and to tailor-make a solution this unique, the problem needs to be precisely identified. This is what we call diagnostic workup. A good diagnostic work up is thorough and aimed at arriving (as close as possible) at one definitive possibility. This is what the clients want because they want the right answer for their pet. This is what your boss wants because she wants you to be productively utilising the diagnostic and surgical facilities of the Practice. This is what You want - weather you already know this or not, because you would rather treat with confidence, then lay awake at night worrying if your one-size-fits-all lucky shot treatment will be successful and what desperate rescue plan you should implement if it's not. Earlier on I said that You, the Veterinary employee, are your boss's biggest liability. The good news is - by using your skills, you can become her biggest, most valuable asset. The choice is up to you.

How To Negotiate a Spectacular Pay Rise

We all want to do rewarding work, be paid well, feel appreciated by our co-workers and our peers. Now, what I am about to tell you will come as a complete shock but trust me on this one - your boss would like to pay you well. Why? Because everyone prefers to work with happy colleagues, not the miserable grumpy ones, with one eye on the 'now hiring' web listings. Any manager will tell you that finding good employees and keeping them is one of the hardest things about running a business, so if you are that reliable, honest, productive employee, your boss will jump through hoops while riding on roller skates backwards just to keep you happy.

So let's say it is the time for your performance review. Or maybe it isn't, but there is this thing, whatever it is, you absolutely need to ask for right now. You are far more likely to be successful in your request if you know how to ask the right way. Like most of us, in order to give you the things that you want, your boss needs to be given a reason. You can give her the reason by building a compelling case. To build a compelling case you need to demonstrate your contribution to clinic productivity, business growth and client satisfaction. Not just talk about it - demonstrate. This means collecting supporting evidence to prove your point. That evidence may be consultation notes, pathology submission forms, customer reviews, etc. It needs to be comparative:

'This is what others do and this is what I do'.

Or

'This is how it was before I started and this is how it is now'.

Or

'This is what I used to do 6 months ago and this is where I am now.'

Your boss is already monitoring the clinic's financial performance so she probably already knows how much on average you earn the clinic per month, per day, per consultation. You may or may not have access to this information. If you do, financial information obviously makes for the best case-building material. If you don't, you will need to extrapolate from other evidence. Maybe it's not pay rise you are after. Maybe you want funded further education or more flexible working hours. The approach is always the same. If you want something extra - you need to demonstrate why you deserve it.

This 'building the case' business sounds like a lot of work. You may ask, does it need to be that hard? Can't I just go to my boss and tell her that I am a really trying to do my best? The answer is, of course it doesn't have to be that hard. Maybe your boss has already decided to give you a pay rise. Maybe she feels sorry for you bringing your home-made sandwiches to work every day instead of buying lunch at the cafe like everyone else. Maybe she likes your new Jimmy Choo handbag so much, she wants to give you more spending power so you can buy another one. Which is great, of course, and makes acing your next performance review dead easy. But that's not the situation I am talking about here. I want you to get that pay rise even if the boss has already decided that you are not getting a dollar more for the next five years. I want you to walk into that office with confidence, knowing that with the hard evidence you have gathered, if your boss does not appreciate how lucky she is to have you as an employee, then the next clinic up the road certainly will. So don't just sit there, start building that case by collecting solid, verifiable, evidence-based portfolio of your financial and customer service success.

Just remember one thing - be honest with yourself. If this evidence was presented to you about another employee, would you feel that the employee is genuinely making an exceptional contribution? Would You give that employee a pay rise (Of course you would, but please for just one minute try to be objective. No really)? There is nothing more annoying than a young upshot thinking that he is god's gift to Veterinary science and the sun rises and sets in his proverbial pants. That's not a way to get a pay rise - that's a guaranteed way to get nothing. Let's say an overconfident rookie of this caliber walks into my office for a performance review. Now, I may think that his performance is deserving of say a 10% pay rise. But if he walks through the door asking for 30% and acting as if he deserves it (not to mention that personalised car spot he has been keeping his eye on), then I am not going to give him the 10% either. I will not give it to him to teach him an important life lesson. I think it was Clint Eastwood who said 'Real heroes talk little and do much'. Or maybe it wasn't Clint Eastwood. The point is, if you ask for what you haven't earned, you make yourself look like a fool. By the way, note I didn't say 'Real heroes say nothing at all'. There are plenty of Veterinarians out there who are getting much less than they deserve, because they never ask. That is wrong too. A good manager will recognise and promote a quiet achiever, but many managers will take advantage of people like that, or they are too busy to notice, or they work on the principle 'if it ain't broken, don't fix it'. So if you think you deserve more, then you should definitely ask. To use a military analogy, if the performance review is an army engagement and each request is a bullet you fire, think of yourself more as an American Sniper type - each bullet is precious but deadly, than the trigger happy Rambo shoot-them-up type (just don't take this analogy too literally - you know what I mean).

Some people fail to get rewarded because they lack self-promotion skills. Other fail because their performance isn't good enough. If you think you may belong in the second category- read on, because the next few chapters may help you improve in ways that will make your boss and your customers very happy.

The Importance of Definitive Diagnosis

Imagine you are visiting a lawyer seeking his help in an important legal matter. As you walk into his office loaded with a pile of legal papers, the lawyer takes one look at you and tells you to put the documents away. You are naturally surprised by this and explain that the documents hold all the intricacies and detail of your important case.

'Don't worry about it.' says the lawyer 'I have been in this game for years, and that little bit of information you gave me on the phone is just enough for me to form a general opinion about your case - enough for me to give a good shot at it. Besides, reviewing all these documents will take hours, and with my steep hourly rate, wouldn't you rather save the money for something else?'

Needless to say, this would be the point where you turn around and start looking for someone else to do the job. A lawyer with that attitude will find few clients. When we consult professionals to solve our problems, we want the problem solved. This naturally includes professionals gaining as much information as they need to enable a solution to be found. It is of little consolation that this specialist's gut feeling is right 80% of the time if you happen to be in the 20% of cases resulting in complete failure.

This is what I find so astonishing about so many expert Veterinarians believing that they are doing their clients a favour by treating a patient having gained an incomplete knowledge database. It is true that clients would prefer to minimise their Veterinary bill. Ideally clients would like to walk in the door, have the Veterinarian wave the magic wand of some kind and watch the problem improve instantly, having paid preferably under $20. Which is a perfectly fine wish to have. I for example would love my mechanic to repair my car in this way, because I don't know anything about cars. But I know that this is impossible, so I leave the car at the repair shop for as long as my mechanic tells me and pay through the nose, because I don't want it to break down in the middle of a long drive.

It is true that our knowledge and experience often allows us to make educated guesses which are usually right most of the time. Despite this, most clients would be horrified if they knew that a serious, albeit uncommon diagnostic differential was not checked for because of the Veterinarian's own mental calculations and without thorough consultation.

As good as we are in our ability to gather clinical history with our hands, eyes and ears, there is no substitute for the necessary laboratory testing to confirm the disease aetiology which you may be already strongly suspecting in your mind.

In the case of a soft tissue mass, for example, there would only be very few instances where a laboratory sample - collected via cytology, punch biopsy or surgical biopsy, would not be indicated in order to form an appropriate care plan. It is simply impossible for a Veterinarian of any skill or experience to make a correct diagnosis without such sample, regardless of the mass's appearance, size, rate of growth, how long it has been there, or how convinced the client is that it looks exactly like another lump his previous dog had eight years ago. Without a sample you just don't know.

Similarly, a case of ear or skin infection cannot be treated with certainty unless an appropriate sample has been collected and examined via cytology or culture - regardless of how suggestive the lesion appearance may be for a particular condition.

Let's say you are presented with an older Cavalier King Charles Spaniel who is coughing, has ascites and an auscultatable left sided systolic heart murmur, you may well suspect mitral valve disease. But that is a suspicion, not a definitive diagnosis. And your suspicion would need to be confirmed by appropriate diagnostic imaging tools for you to be confident in presenting your treatment plan to the client.

Sometimes there are occasions when finding a definitive diagnosis before starting treatment may not be possible. It may be because of money constraints, such as the high cost of brain imaging to differentiate between idiopathic epilepsy and intracranial mass. It may be because it is not possible to conduct follow up visits and the treatment needs to be instituted immediately, such as the case with many semi-feral pets.

Alternatively you may feel that your diagnosis by suspicion is so likely, and the effort and expense of achieving a definitive diagnosis is so great, that treating for the suspected condition would be the appropriate action plan. For example - let's say a dog has vomited twice but shows no other clinical signs, you may feel that treating conservatively for gastroenteritis is the correct approach.

If you do, it is essential that in order to fulfill your duty of care you take the following steps:

You must clearly explain to the client that you suspicion about the patient's condition is just that - a strong suspicion, and that further testing would be necessary to achieve a definitive diagnosis.

You must explain to the client other differentials which may be causing the disease. In our case of suspected gastroenteritis, the vomiting may be caused by intestinal obstruction or metabolic disease among other causes.

You must present the owner with the diagnostic options to differentiate the problem and let them make the choice. In the case of suspected gastroenteritis this may be blood work and abdominal radiographs. Remember - this is not your pet and not your decision to make. You may feel strongly that a particular action plan is the right one to take, but the owner may feel differently.

And finally, you must clearly record you findings, the differential diagnoses, the owner discussion and the treatment decision in you permanent history record.

Following these steps will create happy, satisfied clients by giving them broader knowledge and a sense of being involved in their pet's care. Furthermore, it will greatly reduce the possibility of the client becoming unhappy with your services or pursuing you for clinical negligence through the legal and professional bodies, which should make for a happier Veterinarian - namely You.

Getting back to our example - let's say that vomiting dog came in to be seen by you, it is bright as a button, hungry like a horse, the abdominal palpation is normal and it only vomited twice that morning. You may feel with your hand on your heart that this is 100% guaranteed gastroenteritis case and the conservative approach will fix the problem in two days for sure. That's great and you are probably right. But what if that same dog represents the next day - now it is flat as a pancake, not eating, has vomited every two hours and has an uncomfortable abdomen. Now I see you breaking out in cold sweat, mumbling something about radiographs and thinking about how you can fit in an exploratory laparotomy at 5pm. Now, obviously not all of your cases are going to be like this, hopefully very few will. But the way you have spoken to the client during the first consultation will determine whether these out-of-the-box cases are going to become customer complaint material or not. If you get into the habit of listing differentials and discussing options for all cases - no matter how straightforward they look, you will avoid countless complaints and difficult conversations later.

Some Veterinary legal organisations now say that whenever multiple diagnostic and treatment options exist (which is in almost all cases) a signed confirmation of the treatment choice should be obtained from the owner. At the time of writing I personally have not implemented a system like that. However in the years to come, with the way the litigation world is going, I can see this becoming a necessity in our profession sooner than we would like.

A Word About In-house Laboratory Testing

OK, so if you agree with the part where I talk about how critical it is to reach definitive diagnosis, then you don't need to be reminded that some form of laboratory testing needs to accompany pretty much every medical case that walks in the door.

Most of this laboratory testing can be done in patient-side laboratory setup. Doing it this way has many advantages for the customer and for you. It is much cheaper than sending samples to a pathology lab, you get the results on the spot, and when you look down the microscope and see those eosinophilic bacteria, or those bad nasty cancer cells, it gives you a warm fuzzy feeling because now you've see the enemy, you know exactly how to nail those suckers good. Best of all, if you are not confident with your diagnosis, you can always send the sample on to a pathology lab.

For example, if I am trying to get a definitive diagnosis on a lump, I will always collect and stain an FNA first. Then, if I am not sure what is the type of cells I am looking at, I will happily send the sample to the lab. At least if I can see well preserved cells, I know I will get a diagnosis, not one of those frustrating 'open diagnosis' answers.

A statement I often hear from Veterinarians is that clients decline laboratory testing because it costs too much. If this is what most of your clients say, then I simply don't buy it. Imagine that a shop attendant tells you 'In our store, the more we discount our excellent products, the fewer customers want to purchase them.' Does that statement make sense to you? No, of course it doesn't. Assuming most customers are rational people, it follows that either the product is being hidden out of sight, or the store is doing a poor job explaining the terms of the transaction. So too with laboratory testing. Confirming the diagnosis is not an optional extra - it is the most prudent money saving step you client can make in the treatment of their pet! A cytology test before prescribing antibiotics is more expensive than just antibiotics but it's a whole lot less expensive than another appointment and then a different course of antibiotics.

Therefore a Veterinarian who fails to explain to his client the benefits of diagnostic testing is probably himself lacking the confidence to perform or to interpret these tests. This lack of confidence often exists on a subconscious level with the Veterinarian finding other reasons why the testing only rarely happens.

Here is a simple way you can help yourself break through this psychological barrier: In the next ten medical cases you see, do the in-house laboratory testing (FNA, cytology, trichograms, skin preps, etc.) without charge. You can tell your clients you are doing it and they will love you for it. Or if you are really shy, you can tell them nothing and evaluate the results yourself. Now ask yourself the question - has knowing the result of the test affected my clinical decision making? I guarantee that the answer will be Yes.

You cannot identify the type of bacteria causing the ear infection, nor can you differentiate between bacterial, fungal, parasitic or immune mediated skin condition by just looking at it. You need a cytology sample to do that. It frustrates me beyond limit when clients come with ready-made diagnoses made by Veterinarians at other clinics who have never done any testing at all. This frustration is offset somewhat by the fact that most of those Veterinarians' clients end up leaving in frustration and coming to me instead, at which point I collect a skin scraping or a tape prep and in five minutes present the client with an explanation of what the problem is and how to treat it, which instantly makes me look like a hero in their eyes and other Veterinarian like a complete fool. Naturally, you want to look like a hero too and are therefore keen to use your laboratory skills to look for definitive diagnosis whenever possible. In order to do this effectively you need to feel that your diagnostic skills are providing meaningful information, and that this information can actively contributes to your case management.

First of all, you need to ensure that your in-house laboratory is in good working order and stocked up with the necessary consumables and reagents. Few Veterinarians would be comfortable consulting with a defective stethoscope. Yet many Veterinary clinics I worked at have an old, unusable microscope which hasn't been serviced in years. Without a good microscope a good Veterinarian should feel like a soldier going into battle with a defective rifle. So get yours fixed and serviced by a professional!

Fixing the equipment is the relatively easy part. The hard part is gaining the proficiency and diagnostic skill. This takes time, training and lots of hours of looking down a microscope.

Start by booking yourself some cytology CPD - preferably of the practical variety, not just the sitting in the lecture and listening kind. Then get out your shiny newly serviced microscope and it's sampling time! Start by collecting a sample of every abnormal lesion, not forgetting to look at some normal samples too. Staining and sample preparation takes time and if you are slow at it, you will feel nervous and skip steps so don't try to prepare the sample during a consultation - put them away labelled and view them later. At this point you will not be charging a fee for this service - this is your training time. A great game to play is to make a microscope slide for yourself with every pathology sample you send to the lab. Write down your findings and then compare them to the pathologist's comments when the report comes back. You will know you are making progress when your own notes start sounding as complicated and wordy as the pathology reports.

Of course in-house testing is not a substitute for pathology laboratory. Even for a most skilled clinician there will be times when the tools and the skill set of a specialist Pathologist are essential for a successful treatment. I often find that a Lab report would turn my strong suspicion into a conviction. This is not an admission of failure. Seeking specialist guidance does not expose you as a fraud or demonstrates your limited diagnostic skills in front of clients. Our clients are already familiar and comfortable with this care arrangement based on experiences with their own health, so the idea of external laboratory testing is very natural to them.

To keep the client informed and up to date with their pet's care, don't be afraid to explain how you own diagnostic work up has narrowed down the list of differentials and how a laboratory test would establish the correct diagnosis and ensure that the right treatment is implemented. This after all is what our Veterinary work is all about.

How To Perform A Routine Vaccination

This should be a very quick chapter. Here it goes - perform a clinical exam, draw up the syringe and inject. Right? Not quite. Actually that would be in the chapter 'How *Not* To Perform A Routine Vaccination' - maybe I will put that into my next book. The first thing to understand about a Vaccination is that it is not actually about a Vaccination. The injection happens, of course but that's not how you should be looking at it. A Routine visit - Vaccination or not, I am only using this as an example

- is a precious opportunity. This is your chance to go through all the basics of routine animal husbandry and disease prevention and make sure the client is not missing out on any important components. When the animal presents for a serious health complaint, it is sometimes difficult to raise the issues of routine prevention. If you do start talking about vaccination protocols or the importance of healthy diet in the middle of working up a complex medical case, the client may see you as ignoring their concerns or failing to take them seriously. That's why you save these discussions for a routine health check. In fact many clinics have rebranded their Vaccination visit as 'health assessment' or similar, to emphasise the importance of health review and not just the Vaccination itself.

The first step in performing a good health assessment appointment is the same as the first step in any appointment. No, it's not performing a clinical exam, that happens later. The first thing you must do is familiarise yourself with the patient history and notes by reviewing the CRM. Your computer records contain priceless information and you should try your best never to start any appointment (or even a phone conversation) without reviewing it first.

A good computer system will tell you the basic information about the patient as well as their Vaccination history, use of preventative care, and prescriptions and chronic illnesses, whether the patient may be aggressive, whether the client has an outstanding debt, etc.

Most computer records have a function of pop up notes, so critical information (such as whether the dog will try to bite you) can be displayed instantly without having to scroll through history. You should find that function and get into the habit of using it.

Next, briefly glance over your consulting room to make sure you have everything you need. There is nothing more annoying than having to run out of the consultation room looking for some little thing - like a thermometer or a pen. Whatever is your preferred basic toolkit, make sure it's on hand. Make sure the table is not rocking (don't know about you, but that really annoys me), check that the otoscope cones have been cleaned, make sure you have fresh paper towels, and don't forget to glance over the room to check that the previous patient has not urinated on the door frame while you looked away.

Now open the door and invite your patient in. Make sure you say your name and your patient's name in your first sentence. Something like

'Hi, I am Doctor Vadim. It's great to see Fluffy today.'

Clients love to hear their pets' name but they *need* to hear your name. Even if you are wearing your name tag, the clients don't know how to refer to you. If you name is not very common, like mine, they will be afraid of pronouncing it incorrectly. Even if your name is easy to pronounce, they still don't know what you prefer to be called. Should they call you Dr John or Dr Smith or Dr John Smith? Make their life easier by telling them in the first sentence.

When calling the client in, don't stand in the consulting room - walk out into the waiting area and welcome them in. The beginning of any consultation is a moment of anxiety. The client is not sure of what is about to happen next. Put them at ease by smiling, making eye contact and looking approachable.

Make sure you take and record the animal's weight. Many clinics place the walk-on scales in the waiting room and by the time client is called in, the nurse has already measured the weight and recorded it into the patient's file. This is a great practice to follow. The client may be nervous of the weight-in, either because their pet is overweight or afraid of the scales, so you may need to help them.

Naturally, from the moment you open the door, you would be observing the patient's general appearance, movement and demeanor. Before you actually get back into the consultation room, you should already know if your patient is healthy weight, limping, anxious, has any obvious skin conditions, etc.

Once you are back in the room, acknowledge the reason for the visit:

'I see Fluffy is due for a Vaccination.'

And then give the client permission to communicate to you any health concerns they may have:

'Let me know if there are any specific concerns or problems with Fluffy you want me to check.'

This is the point where you keep quiet, don't interrupt and let the client talk. Once the client has finished, clarify any points unclear to you by saying it back to them and asking to clarify:

'So Fluffy had diarrhoea for two weeks?'

I prefer to gather as much of the patient history as I can before examining the patient so that I can use the information during the clinical exam.

Once you are confident you got the full history - perform the clinical exam.

I am not going to waste time teaching the skill of clinical examination here. We all do it a little differently following the sequence that works for us best. The only point I will make is to develop your own sequence and follow it every time without fail. You are much less likely to miss or skip things that way, especially if you are tired, in a rush or just not having a good day.

If the client indicated a particular concern to me, such as a lump or ocular discharge, I will examine that area first, acknowledge the concern and then begin my usual clinical examination sequence as I always do.

This is purely to validate the client's concern about that particular problem. Imagine you just spent ten minutes talking about Fluffy's limping, only to have the Veterinarian approach Fluffy and start taking his temperature. You don't know that this Veterinarian starts all his clinical examinations with temperature taking and that he is well aware and intent on thoroughly assessing the lameness in due time, so you may well feel that your important health concern has been not listened to.

As part of your clinical examination, make sure you are acknowledging and verbalising your findings to the client. This includes both normal and abnormal findings. Let's say you are examining a six months old puppy, you can comment for example on how good his ears look. Sure, most puppies of this age have great ears, sure you have seen lots of puppies' ears this week and they all look pretty much the same to you. Just remember -

the client doesn't know any of that and by mentioning how clean the ears are, you will make their day. They will be telling everyone in the dog park just how healthy their puppy's ears are and how great the Vet is who told them so. They will probably remember this a year later and will be waiting for a comment from you about ears at their next annual vaccination. Moreover, if a year or two later you do mention to them that the ears have too much discharge, they will be super committed to implementing the best preventative care to fix the problem as soon as possible - and they will be looking to you to tell them how to do it.

If a problem was identified on the history or the clinical exam - make sure you provide a plan. The plan may include further diagnostic work, it may include treatment or preventative care steps. Whatever you advise, make sure the client knows what they need to do, when and what the final objective is. If a follow up visit is needed, this is the time to book it.

If the patient is healthy and well, that is great, but you still need a plan - a plan how to keep it that way. It may include diet changes, advice on appropriate levels and type of exercise, other preventative care steps (cleaning ears, wiping between skin folds), grooming advice, etc.

The next part is to review the parasite prevention currently being used by the client. A good CRM will alert you to any glaring gaps in prevention, like the client who hasn't bought intestinal worming treatment for two years. Then again, he may be buying it on the internet or at a pet shop. So ask a sufficiently open ended questions to let the client explain the protocol himself.

'So, what are you using to treat Fluffy's intestinal worms?' is a better question than:

'When did you last treat Fluffy's worms?' Which has a distinctly inquisitorial feel and is much more likely to elicit a defensive response.

The type of preventative care that is necessary will obviously depend on the geographic factors and the pet's actual situation.

In large parts of Europe and America you would be worried about Heartworm, whereas in the Middle East you would be more concerned about Parkworm.

What you are aiming for, once again is to have the owner walk out of the clinic with a clear parasite prevention plan. There are many products available, so it's not enough to just list the products. This has the effect of just confusing people more. You need to tell the client what type/frequency/route of treatment is preferable to them and then point them to the exact product which they need. Ideally they should be taking this product home with them on the day, so as to make the whole process clear and easy to follow.

When multiple products with similar applications are available, my preference is always to recommend the product administered or available through the clinic, simply because when it comes to regular treatments, most people will sometimes forget and the clinic reminder can make the difference between the pet having the protection or being exposed to disease.

Once you have covered preventative care, don't forget to discuss diet. A discussion about diet should be an integral part of all your wellness consultations. We live in the day and age when most medical conditions have tailor made, scientifically validated diets to assist treatment. Those animals without a medical condition can also benefit from a diet which reflects their built, lifestyle and exercise factors.

Many Veterinarians mistakenly believe that by promoting diets they will be somehow seen as hard selling or cheapening the value of their advice. In my experience the opposite is true. Clients love getting food advice from a Veterinarian. They see food as a natural, safe medicine, which can enhance whatever other treatment tools they may be trying to implement. Moreover, getting advice from you saves them from the need of staring at the supermarket shelves where dozens of brightly coloured bags with smiling dogs and cats are staring back at them. Just remember, when you make a dietary recommendation, you are doing your customer a great service.

Ok, we finally got to the bit when you actually do the vaccination. Don't forget to reiterate when the next vaccination needs to be done and to set the appropriate reminders for the vaccination and other components of preventative care.

You may think that the visit is over and you can bid your client goodbye and escort them out of the consultation room. But there is another important step you must do.

This is where you walk out with the client into the waiting area and show (by picking up and handling) the preventative care products, food recommendations and other healthcare aides which you recommended during the consultation.

Remember, all the things that you said are just fancy long words to you client. Now they have been let out, they are again alone on their own in front of a shelf full of colourful bags and boxes. You need to physically point out to them the actual products you talked about so that your good recommendations don't remain just that.

How To Resolve Client Complaints

Resolving complaints is the task everyone hates. I am hoping that by taking to heart all the things I wrote in the processing chapters, you will have fewer complaints in the first place. That being said, of course, you could be the most amazing, knowledgeable, caring Veterinarian on the face of this earth but you can't eliminate all complaints no matter how hard you try.

Some people like to complain and do it frequently and for petty reasons. Others bear the disagreements silently, only complain when they perceive that a monstrous injustice has been perpetrated against them.

Whatever the reasons, I guarantee you that amongst you administrative and clinical tasks, customer complaint resolution would consume a disproportionately large amount of time and energy.

No one likes complaint resolution work and I am no exception. But having worked in complaint resolution, I see this field as not just a giant nuisance and pain in the backside, but as a unique opportunity.

First of all, it's an opportunity to improve. If there were no complaints, we wouldn't know which areas of business we need to try harder in. Secondly, it's an opportunity to set yourself and your business apart in a good way. Sure, everyone is all smiles when everything is going well. But when the system fails, that's when you can show the client the meaning of 'above and beyond' and turn an occasional customer into the one who is bonded for life. The main thing is to remove from yourself the feelings of guilt and anger. Think about it - do you get angry at an aggressive neoplasia or a difficult fracture? No, of course you don't. Challenging cases are a part of our job. We use our clinical tools and experience to solve it to the best of our abilities. Complaint resolution is no different. It's a challenging part of our job, but we can rise to that challenge.

Even though every complaint is unique, I have somewhat of a template approach to complaint resolution and here it is:

- Choose the time and location wisely. If you know that the customer is seeking your time to air a complaint, don't try and address it during a five minute break between consultations while standing in the corridor. Try to allocate a time when you will not be disturbed, and a place away from foot traffic. If you have been 'ambushed' by an angry customer, simply explain that you want to allocate appropriate time to address the concern properly and make a time for a proper meeting.

- Prepare in advance. Before meeting the angry customer speak to all the staff members involved and read all case notes thoroughly. You want to build as much of a complete picture of the situation as you possibly can.

- Ask the client to explain the situation in detail. Listen attentively and make notes if you need to. Do not interrupt or try to correct the customer based on other sources you may have available. Wait a few seconds after the customer has finished speaking before speaking yourself.

- Summarise the substance of the complaint as you understood it back to the customer. Use an expression similar to:

  'So the way I understand it this is what happened..'

- As you are summarising the substance of the complaint back to the customer, make sure to differentiate objective facts ('What happened is...') from feelings and interpretations ('The way it made you feel is...'). Feelings are very important and legitimate, but they are different from facts.

- Apologise to the customer. Very few complaints do not require an apology. An apology is not a sign of weakness nor is it an admission of guilt. Even when you feel that you and your staff have done nothing wrong, an apology can serve as a simple acknowledgement of the client's distress:

  'I am sorry that this is how the situation made you feel.'

- Ask the customer what kind of resolution he or she may have in mind. By this point you may already have a mental picture of how the problem needs to be addressed.

Don't rush with the judgement. You may be surprised how the customer's view of the situation may greatly differ from your own.

- Propose a resolution of your own. Be positive and solution focused. Use the language similar to:

  'Ms Smith, here is how I think we can solve the problem...'

- Discuss the solution with the customer to find the win-win. Obviously the solution will depend on where in your opinion the responsibility for the problem lies and whether you feel that the customer's requests are reasonable or not. However, there is one thing you and the customer both want to achieve - you both want a speedy and satisfactory solution to the problem. The problem is not the person - the problem is the situation. By approaching the conflict in this way you will find it easier to find a resolution that suits everyone.

- Review the procedures. Once an acceptable resolution has been found, don't just stop there. Use this as a learning opportunity to make sure a similar problem does not arrive again. Review you own steps or speak with your colleagues if you need to. Make a record about the problem and the resolution to it as part of appropriate incident recording and patient notes. Real life difficulties are some of the best ways for us to improve and learn.

The Basics of Veterinary Marketing

If you think of marketing only as paying for advertising to promote your business, then unless you are a business owner, you don't need to know anything about marketing. And if you are a business owner, then you would be hiring a marketing expert to do it for you, because marketing is a job for marketers, right? If you think that, you would be completely wrong. Because marketing is what all of us do all the time. Marketing ourselves and our work, that is. We all want to be liked, make a good impression, stand out from the crowd. On the job, at an interview or at a dinner party. The way we are doing this, consciously or not, is by trying to maximise our good qualities in the eyes of others, and make them remember those qualities, which is what marketing really is. So having basic understanding of how marketing works will help you at every point of your life - professional and otherwise.

Dinner party conversation aside, as a practicing Veterinarian, you want your personal Veterinary brand to be unique and to stand for something. Your employer Practice may well have its' own professional identity and you may naturally want to uphold that identity but doing that is in no way incompatible with developing your own unique professional brand and identity. Because after all you are not a robot or a clone and the way you work is going to be unique in its' own way, so that just as you want your clients to say 'I go to So-and-so Clinic', you also want your clients to say proudly 'I go to Doctor so-and-so' - which means you personally. This is obviously beneficial to you if you are running your own business, but it is just as beneficial to you if you are a practice employee, because the clients who like you and want to be seen by you are happier, more satisfied clients, which makes for a more satisfied, less anxious, happier Veterinarian, and that is you.

They say the best marketing is word of mouth marketing. Have you heard that? Me too. It's like one of those statements you can throw out there without any need for a clarification follow up. After all, what can we do to control and influence word of mouth? Well, trying not to do anything embarrassingly wrong, obviously. But what about beyond that? It turns out we can do a lot.

The overall principle goes something like this: in your clients' mind there is a mental picture of what their experience at the Vet's should be like. On the most basic level, the client has a need or a problem and they are hoping to have this need met/problem solved by the time they walk out the door. Got that. So is that how you generate good word of mouth? Not at all. Actually on the word of mouth scale just getting the job done gets you exactly to the 'zero' mark, which in these days of trolling and hate speech is already an achievement.

If you have avoided creating any negative experiences and associations in your client's mind, then you are unlikely to generate any negative reviews and suggestions to the client's friends and family as well as on the social media. Well done to you for that. But you don't just want to avoid negative referrals, right? You are aiming higher than that. You want positive ones, and lots of them. To do that you need to do more than just fix the client's problem.

An un-memorable experience creates no positive memories. So to create a positive memory, the kind of experience the client will feel happy to share with their family and friends, you need to exceed their expectations. The great news is, there are countless ways in which you can do that.

Let's ask ourselves - what does the client want? They want their pet to be looked after, they want to be educated, they want to feel a connection - with you, with the rest of the clinic staff, with the clinic itself. They want to feel that they are more than just a customer in a line of other customers.

A study of human medical specialists has found that those specialists least likely to have complaints raised against them are not the most skilled or experienced, but the ones who have spent a few minutes extra talking with their patients. So let's take a leaf out of their book.

Clients know that we Veterinarians are busy and overworked. They feel profound gratitude when we stop and discuss their situation and their pet's in great detail. Nothing generates better word of mouth reviews then a perception of Veterinarian as being a good and caring communicator. Our best marketing tool is located just above our chin and below our nose. And it doesn't cost a cent to operate, except a little spare time. So let's use it to its maximum potential.

In my experience, the only thing clients like more than the Veterinarian's communication is *unexpected* communication - communication at times other than scheduled appointment times. On the phone, between consultations and so on. This is obviously the time we also find precious - our opportunity to review cases, write notes and just catch a breath on a busy day. So the natural inclination is often to put up a wall and push the client away. This is understandable and the boundaries between personal and work time need to be respected. But don't think of this as wasted time. Just because there is no dollar value doesn't mean there is no intangible value. If marketing is going an extra step, then this is marketing at its' best. Nor does it always have to be unpaid time. Consider scheduling in 'unplanned' customer discussions for those clients most likely to benefit from this. You can factor the cost of this into other fees. After all, a premium service can command a premium price.

Intangible communication value is also regarded higher by clients then dollar value. Or, to put the same idea differently, there is a measurable financial premium a professional can charge for enhanced customer communication.

It is falsely believed by many Veterinarians that price discount is the main parameter customers look for. In fact in numerous customer surveys show that the cost of service rates lower in the customers' mind then many other intangible factors.

Moreover, customers earned on the strength of discounts alone are unlikely to stay around the moment the Clinic is perceived to no longer provide the cheapest value. On the other hand, a Clinic reputed for communication and customer service will overcome transient challenges and retain a loyal client base even when external circumstances change.

This is not to understate the power of a discount as a tool to enhance your relationship with the customer. A discount is a powerful gesture of goodwill. It's like a special gift you bestow on the special people you choose to show favour to.

In the marketing terms a discount can be used in one of two ways - as a tool to reach new customers or to reward existing ones. In either case a discount can only do its' job if it is seen as a special and unique value. The customer needs to know what the real value of the service is and that they are getting a special and time limited offer. In order to do this effectively you need to inherently recognise and believe in your Clinic's and your own Professional Value - if you don't believe in it yourself, how can you possibly communicate it to your customer! (If so, consider re-reading the Professional Value chapter of this book).

When you fail to explain the discount value to the client, you haven't actually used a marketing tool. You have simply taken you Clinic's money and flushed it down the toilet. Or burned it in a little bonfire. Or whatever other visual demonstration works for you best to make that point.

In fact, it's worse than that. Giving away your service for a reduced price didn't only deprive your Clinic of so many dollars and cents. It has also diminished the value of your service in your client's eyes and has created an expectation for the future. The client will naturally expect the service for the same low price next time and the time after that. And if the price becomes suddenly more, he will feel justifiably upset and you will need to review the 'Resolving Customer Complaints' chapter of this book. He will also tell his friends and when they come to visit the Clinic, they too will expect the lower price and feel short changed when they do not receive it.

So instead of making yourself look good, you have now created a whole lot of negative word of mouth about how you Clinic's pricing is excessive, unfair and arbitrary. And all you needed to do is to demonstrate the value of the Discount and to present it as special and valuable. At the very least, the full price and the value of the discount need to appear on the invoice. It is even better to verbally explain how the actual price is calculated, what discount is being applied and how much it is saving for the customer.

I routinely turn the computer screen towards the customer during the billing process and explain exactly what different components on the bill are and how they are calculated. Rather than creating tension, this makes the customer feel more informed about the billing process and ultimately about the value of the service itself. And as I keep saying all the time, an informed client is always more likely to be a satisfied client.

Word of mouth is great but what about external marketing? We all understand the marketing value of getting our business publicised in the media. The problem is, advertising space is expensive and most of us have by now become conditioned to pay as little attention to it as we possibly can. How much attention do you devote to print media advertising or the annoying pop up ads on the web? We all can recall the big brand marketing campaigns, of course.

But this kind of marketing is usually out of the average Veterinarian's reach.

The truth is, there is a powerful advantage we hold over almost all other business enterprises. For reasons largely unclear to me, most people find our line of work absolutely fascinating. Just count how many times you will be asked about the work you do at the next family gathering or dinner party. Most of us, myself included find this attention quite annoying at times. But you can turn this to your advantage by turning your work stories into marketing value.

It's called Content Marketing. To do this you will need, you guessed it - content, and media contacts. Just as importantly, the one thing you usually don't need is large amounts of money.

So how do you get content? Well, think about your average work day. The things you find routine and trivial, others will find unexpectedly fun and exciting. It helps to talk with you non-Veterinary friends just to gauge what they find cute, entertaining or disgusting. In any content format a photo will always help. So having a photo-taking technology handy (a camera, tablet, smart phone) is always a good idea. Then, once you've got your story, you need to put it into words. A professional writer will do this well. But you may well surprise yourself what you can do with a bit of practice. Remember, the more you write, the better you get at writing. The story doesn't need to be long - in fact shorter is often better. It just needs to be positive, have a sense of character and a happy ending.

Once you have written your story, you need to get it out into the media. Paper or digital, the way you determine if the medium is right for you is by asking how many eyeballs are looking at it and are they 'relevant eyeballs' ie. viewers with the potential of becoming your customers. A media platform with thousands of views is no good to you if the viewers are geographically removed from your Clinic or are unlikely to have pets. That being said, the principle of 'any publicity is good publicity' does apply to some extent. Sometimes referrals can come from very unusual places.

Once you've picked out the right media platform - make contact with the journalist/writer/content manager and start a conversation. Don't be afraid to offer what you have, just put yourself into the journalist's shoes. Every week the designated media pages need to be filled. With the number of news/entertainment sources exploding in recent years, journalists are always on the lookout for good stories. So they are not doing you a favour any more then you are doing a favour for them.

And in return for your content, journalists are usually happy to provide your and your Clinic's contact details. That's the implied understanding - the media reference is the return for your hard work. Sometimes you will even get paid. I have found that by pitching stories for marketing publicity I would occasionally get a cheque in the mail, and wouldn't we all like that.

Managing Your Time

If you work in the practice like the one I work in, there is always more work you could be doing. My roster of consulting and surgery times is always booked up. Customers call in to book in appointments and procedures, while there are appointment times available. Once there are no appointments available - some people can be seen at other times and others can't, so they become double bookings. This is not counting emergency cases which obviously come without an appointment.

Then there are phone calls. Customers call wanting to talk about pathology results, hospital cases and general advice of all kinds. That doesn't get time allocated on the daily schedule.

And what about paperwork tasks. The Controlled Substances register needs to be kept up to date, Insurance certificates filled out, letters and email communication answered.

This is all just the clinical work - the bread and butter of the Veterinary business. If you are a manager like me, you also have to find time for management tasks - monitoring the financial performance of the Practice, business meeting etc.

So just as I said, I could easily stay at work all day and all night and still have work left to do. So how do we manage all of those conflicting work demands while still maintaining a normal life? Let me share with you some of the tricks I found have worked for myself.

Mission Statement is a business management concept that used to be popular until quite recently and fell out of favour somewhat in the last few years. The idea is that every company or business is meant to have a Mission Statement - a one line declaration defining what exactly the business is all about.

Every business task - no matter how big or small, whether it is performed by the doorman or the CEO, is supposed to feed back into the Mission Statement.

I for one was disappointed when the whole Mission Statement movement fell out of favour with the Management community. Because we all could do with a Mission Statement of our own.

Take me for example - I am a Veterinary clinician and a business manager. But I am also married with five kids (and expecting kid number six as I am writing this). I need to maintain and improve my Veterinary clinical skills, my customer service skills and my management skills. These are all very important because they support my ability to perform my work properly, and that in turn is very important because it underpins my ability to provide for and look after my family. That's the way I see it. Imagine if it was the other way around. If your work tasks overtake your family and your life on your priorities ladder - you would be completely missing the point.

Your personal Mission Statement in your head needs to reflect your hierarchy of priorities. In turn, that hierarchy of priorities needs to inform your actions. Once you are clear in your head what your priorities are, that clarity will start filtering down to your smallest tasks. It takes time to happen and sometimes you find yourself stuck interminably on the most meaningless and futile tasks. This is very frustrating but at least you begin to understand where the changes in your life need to be made. Knowing what needs to be changed is the first step to making that change. Maybe you need to improve your efficiency, or book out more admin time on your roster, or start looking for another job. That's your choice to ponder, but where you start is with a mental picture of what your time flow should be like.

Multitasking. Oh that wonderful word. Are you are multitasker? I know I am not. In fact, I am as incapable of multitasking as any person you will ever meet. And yet I am a very productive person. I wrote this book while managing two clinics, working as a head Veterinarian and raising a family of five. I think that's impressive. How did I do it? By making a conscious effort to avoid all multitasking!

You see, as Veterinarians we are bombarded with multiple tasks and pieces of information all the time. Some of this information is absolutely critical, such as an emergency walking in the door in the middle of a Vaccination appointment. Most of this information is completely unimportant and can be addressed later.

Have you ever played the computer game SIMs? It was all the rage in the 1990s so if you are from that generation like me, you probably just about lived in it. And if you are younger than that, you probably don't know what I am talking about. In the game you have virtual human characters engaged in various life-like tasks. You give them new tasks to do and the tasks appear as a little emoji string on top of your computer screen. As the characters do the tasks, the emojis fall away and you need to add new ones. If the character finished all his tasks, he just stands there like a work experience kid with nothing to do.

I didn't know it back then, but when I was playing that game as a high school kid, that was good practice because now I pretty much live my life that way. I have a string of tasks in my head and each time a new task comes in I quickly check if it's urgent enough for me to interrupt what I am doing. If not, then I slot it nearly amongst other to-do tasks in order of priorities.

Let's say I am putting a catheter into a dehydrated dog, and on the table nearby I have a set of blood results to look at and a muffin with a cup of tea to drink when I have a chance (priorities list: catheter, blood test, muffin). Then a nurse comes in with a desexing certificate for me to sign. I tell her to put the certificate on the table and I will sign it soon (priorities: catheter, blood test, certificate, muffin). Then a phone call comes in about a cat stung by a bee. So I tell the nurse to hold onto the catheter dog while I speak on the phone. The tea on the table is getting colder (priorities: phone call, catheter, blood test, certificate, muffin). While I am on the phone, I get to sign the desexing certificate and the nurse has finished dressing the catheter - we are making great progress here (priorities: blood test, muffin). Then the receptionist sticks her head through the door and says that a vaccination walk-in appointment has just arrived. I tell her to ask the appointment to take a seat for 10 minutes, quickly make notes about the blood test while scoffing down the muffin, and in 8.5 minutes I call the appointment in, all caught up and feeling ready to conquer the world.

Note - no multitasking here!

If you know your day is going to be hectic (and for some of us those are called work days), advanced planning and organisation can make all the difference between a busy day and a complete disaster.

- Book intelligently. If a skin or an ear problem is booked in - allocate enough time to cover the necessary in-house laboratory work.

- Teach your nurses/receptionists to book intelligently too. All appointments are different but some basic rule of thumb guidelines (stitches out - 10 minutes, vaccinations - 20 minutes, medical work ups - 30 minutes) can be easy to apply by anyone. Write the guidelines down, laminate it and stick in on the front desk so everyone can see.

- Bring a drink bottle and keep it next to you. On a busy day getting to the kitchen to get a drink may be a bridge too far. So fight dehydration be having the drink at hand.

- Pack convenient meal options. A pack of crackers or a soup-in-a-cup is easier to eat on the run than a sandwich and salad.

- Carry your tools onboard. There is nothing more annoying then hunting for a pair of scissors or a pen in the middle of a medical emergency. So keep your favourite tools on you. I carry a little belt pouch with a calculator, scissors, pen, hemostats and a note book. This is especially useful if you are working in an unfamiliar clinic and don't know where everything is.

- Keep a brief to-do running sheet. You know how earlier I spoke about a mental string of things to do in my head, well it works even better if you write them down. It only needs to be one or two words on paper to jog your memory. You can teach your nurses to add to it too, which means one less thing for you to worry about.

- Fit little tasks around big ones. A lot of tasks which fill our day are little niggling things of low importance, which nevertheless need to be done right now (yesterday). They usually don't require much thought but when added up, they can take up surprisingly large amount of your time. Try fitting then in between the larger, more mentally demanding duties. You can sign certificates while waiting for a centrifuge to finish spinning, fill out drug registers while listening to the on-hold phone music and keep tabs on pharmacy stock levels in between consultations. Every little task you get out of the way is one less thing to do at the end of the day.

- Try hard to not leave the tasks unfinished. Resist the urge to drop a task half way when a seemingly more important task arrives. Most things are not so urgent that they can't wait for a few minutes. Leaving a task half-finished is often the same as having to do it again. I try my best to avoid having to exert the mental effort needed to pick up your trail of thought and work out what has and hasn't been done already.

- Make sure you write your consultation notes on the day. Unless you have photographic memory, make a rule to never leave history writing till next day. There are few things I recommend staying after work for, but this is one of them. If you leave history writing till tomorrow, your recall will be limited, you will omit important facts and potentially expose yourself to unnecessary risks. You can make brief, point form notes to expand upon later. But make sure you write down at least the briefest outline as soon as possible.

- Professional Development is very important for Veterinarians and can take a lot of your time, but there are now many more ways to do it then sitting inside lecture theatre listening to someone talk. Webinar learning is becoming increasingly popular. You don't need to travel anywhere and most webinars are recorded so you can watch them at the time best for you. You can listen to audio files - in the car or on public transport. You can fill out quizzes at the end of scientific articles in Veterinary magazines to receive Board approved CPD points.

Above all, always remember that all tasks are not equal. Some tasks are of critical nature and failing to complete those may have a catastrophic effect on you career or personal life. If you take a moment thinking about it, you will realise that these tasks are actually very few in number. Most of the tasks we spend worrying about are actually of the petty, unimportant variety. We would be much better served by gaining the necessary perspective to see those tasks as they are - tiny humps on the road to our important destination. The real danger is not failing to give them due attention - the real danger is exerting unnecessarily our valuable energy reserves and failing to see the road ahead.

Maintaining Your Emotional Health

It is increasingly recognised that compared to other professions, Veterinarians are at a disproportionality greater risk of self-harm. The statistical data has been available for a very long time but it is only recently that this is being openly discussed within the profession.

To put it bluntly, too many Vets are killing themselves, which is unacceptable, tragic and needs to be addressed by the profession urgently, on every level and as a matter of highest priority!

It is becoming more common to see medical health experts invited to speak at Veterinary conferences and to hear encouragements for those at risk to contact suicide prevention services etc.

These are of course great developments and all efforts should be made to promote those. However, ridiculously little is being done to teach Veterinarians how to maintain their emotional health and thus to try and prevent the emergence of suicide related thoughts and behaviours in the first place. Surely if we choose to passionately recommend preventative care for our clients and their pets, then we could be just as passionate about promoting preventative emotional health within ourselves!

This chapter is not a self-help guide for those contemplating suicide - people in that situation should immediately contact professional suicide prevention services.

My aim in this chapter is to provide overview of some of the emotional health improvement tools and how they apply in Veterinary context, as based on my personal research and experience.

First of all, we must recognise that the very nature of our profession puts us into a high risk category for anxiety and depression. This is not to be confused with a separate concern related to the Profession's easy access to lethal drugs.

Other professions have similar rates of emotional distress, but without the means being so readily available, their suicide rates are much lower. In the Veterinary profession within the larger subset of individuals struggling with mental health issues, a small subset may find it easier to act out on these issues in the form of self-harm.

What this means is that putting stricter barbiturate control measures in place (such as requiring two people to unlock the safe every time euthanasia drug is required) may well reduce the rate of suicides, which is a positive development. But that is in no way addressing the underlying emotional ill health, which is the cause of the problem in the first place.

Much has been said about the multiple factors within the profession creating the recipe for emotional stress.

High responsibility, long hours, compassion fatigue and many other factors probably all contribute to some degree. Although some incremental improvements can probably be made (managing work hours, decreasing the numbers of euthanasia per practitioner), it seems likely that the bulk of these factors cannot be eliminated from the profession.

So if the very nature of our work exposes us to increased emotional risk, it naturally follows that we must take proactive steps to mitigate and manage that risk, in a similar way that the profession mitigates and manages the risk of radiation exposure and inhaled anaesthetic agents, rather than waiting for symptoms of radiation poisoning or chemical toxicity to occur and then treating that as a medical illness.

Throughout my career I have struggled with depression and anxiety. When I discussed those concerns with doctors, which I did on multiple occasions, their recommendation was usually different forms of counselling and 'talk therapy'. I always found counselling somewhat helpful in the short term, but the benefits rarely lasted beyond few months post therapy sessions. In addition to seeking professional help I also did a great deal of personal study in the field and experimented with behaviour and lifestyle changes. None of this, I might add involved experimenting with any chemical substances. Slowly, over the course of 15 years I developed a combination of lifestyle and mental health changes which improved my mental state and allowed me to maintain this improvement long term.

Emotional health begins with healthy lifestyle. The foundation of healthy lifestyle is healthy and regular meals, regular exercise and sufficient sleep. This may appear a trivial thing to say but many professionals, not just Veterinarians, underestimate the importance these component play in creating a foundation of good emotional health.

We live in a society and a culture where temporal functions are seen as divorced from our physical selves. As intellectuals trained in Western tradition of thought, Veterinarians are especially prone to not see their physical state as impacting on their ability to evaluate situations and make decisions.

We all accept that physical fitness is helpful when performing orthopaedic surgery or that fatigue can impact on our ability to make split second decisions in an emergency setting. But what about the impact on how positively we view our day or how stressful we find a euthanasia or an encounter with a difficult client.

Our physical state impacts on every decision and every though we have in our day, and this impact is completely unrecognised by us in the same way as a drunk person is unable to recognise the impact alcohol has on his reaction time.

What are the ingredients of healthy lifestyle? Here I am not going to say anything you haven't heard before, but I am saying it anyway because so many people are struggling to accept this message when they are hearing it.

Adequate sleep means eight hour a night of uninterrupted sleep in bed.

Healthy nutrition means three nutritionally balanced meals a day (coffee doesn't qualify as a nutritious meal).

Regular exercise means daily exercise.

Swallowing pieces of chocolate between consultations and sleeping on a chair in a spare examination room does not qualify as healthy lifestyle, despite what your boss may be telling you.

Implementing the basics of healthy lifestyle has a dual effect. For those who are currently emotionally healthy and not in need of additional help, it will cushion the ups and downs of your life and help keep it that way. For those who may be in need of or are already receiving other forms of help for emotional difficulties, it will make those other forms of help much more effective.

Meditation/mindfulness. Both words mean the same thing. Among the self-help tools recommended to Veterinarians including myself, this one is mentioned most commonly and has become a bit of a buzzword in the profession and the society at large. Mindfulness used to be taught in face to face classes. These days there are countless mindfulness-like tools offered online and over various mobile platforms. It's easy to see why this method may seem well suited to Veterinarians. It is self-paced, takes little time and doesn't carry the expense of face-to-face therapy. There is also strong evidence that meditation does have real and measurable health benefits. I was taught meditation ten years ago and practice it regularly. It is a great addition to whatever armoury of other emotional assistance tools you may be carrying in your mental toolbox. However, I believe it is important to be clear about what meditation can and cannot do, and in what context it may be helpful.

First of all, to be of assistance, meditation needs to be practiced regularly - and not only in times of stress, but as a routine activity akin to an exercise program.

Then, we must be clear about what meditation is doing - namely it is a tool to relieve stress. Stress is an emotion but it is also a physical state. When we are stressed, we think differently and we also feel differently. Most importantly, we do not realise when this is happening to us. Stress stops us from thinking straight and it can physically harm our bodies. Stress is a feedback loop, once we are in it it's hard to get out because the physical sensation of stress is in itself a stress inducing factor.

Meditation helps us to break this feedback loop. It helps to combat the physical symptoms of stress as well as the lack of emotional clarity. As such, it is a very important and useful tool. But it cannot combat the *causes* of stress.

Stress comes about when we feel we are under some kind of physical or emotional attack. You know the story - a caveman is chased by a sabre toothed tiger one all that. To make a clean getaway the caveman's body needs to work at full capacity - the heart pumping, the blood vessels dilating and so on. So the theory goes that a little bit of stress is good for us. But if it happens constantly, our bodies cannot work well under that kind of pressure.

The problem is, what if you *think* that the sabre tooth tiger is chasing you, and you think it all the time. You think you are an inadequate clinician, you think your colleagues dislike you, you think your life is going in circles, you think any one of countless negative things people think to themselves. It will make you stressed and anxious. If you use meditation, it will make you less stressed, but it wouldn't take away your thoughts so the stress will come back very quickly.

For some people the anxiety is the problem. For them meditation may be the main part of the solution. But these people are the minority. For most people the feelings of depression and anxiety are driven by depressive and anxious thoughts. For them meditation will help too, but only within the framework of a broader treatment, and this treatment needs to somehow address the harmful and destructive thought patterns, which drive the condition.

One such approach is Cognitive Behaviour Therapy (CBT). This form of therapy is very popular among counselors and psychiatrists and is delivered in a number of forms. Ultimately it is a therapy aimed at identifying unhealthy thought patterns and replacing them with healthier ones. Traditionally it would be delivered in a counselling/therapy session where the patient would be asked questions about how they feel and the councilor would identify thought patterns and teach the patient how to change them.

If meditation can be seen as improving the unhealthy feelings, CBT is the equivalent for improving the unhealthy thoughts. The two can be viewed as working hand in hand and improving each other.

Recently a number of very good online programs have become available. These work by asking the user to complete extensive questionnaires and then apply algorithms to diagnose the problem and lead the user towards a solution.

Naturally, a well trained and experienced councilor would be far more effective than any software. However many people may find face to face counselling uncomfortable, time consuming or expensive. For those an online alternative may be very helpful.

Having interacted with a number of online CBT options I have found them surprisingly helpful. At the time of writing, the most impressive program I have found is Mood gym, found at:

https://moodgym.anu.edu.au/

It is a free, self-paced online service provided by the Australian National University. I feel that every Veterinarian at any stage of their career would benefit from participating in a program like this.

Now I have briefly explained to you what CBT is, I am going to describe a different method which - just to confuse you, tries to achieve exactly the opposite. I am going to call it Anti-CBT. If CBT is all about rationally disproving your self-destructive inner thoughts, Anti-CBT tells you to stop wasting your time. Surely you could fight every one of those thoughts with oodles of persuasive logic, but that's a very emotionally draining battle, and a battle which you ultimately never win. The more killer arguments you present, the more counter arguments your destructive inner self will present in return, after all there is no objective referee living in your head, is there?

So Anti-CBT tells you to stop fighting and recognise that these thought are just that - thoughts. They do not make physical reality. All you need to do is recognise them and acknowledge that they (the thoughts) are separate from you - the person.

To help me illustrate this, picture yourself at a warm sunny beach, knee deep in beautiful, clear ocean. You are enjoying the scene, eyes closed, sun on your cheeks, suddenly a beach ball comes flying out of nowhere and hits you right on the head. Instantly your pleasant mood is gone you feel the flush of anger. You grab the offending ball and push it hard under the water, trying to make it disappear out of sight. You are no longer enjoying yourself and instead you are working hard to keep the ball out of the picture as it tries to bob up from below the waves, over here, than over there, then somewhere else.

The ball is the negative thoughts bobbing up in your head. Instead of trying to push it away, wouldn't it be easier to just let it float on the ocean surface paying altogether little attention to it? Even as I am writing these words, I am reminded just how easy it is for me to say this and how increasingly, astonishingly hard this is to implement. Moreover, this little story begs the question: so how do you know when you should push the beach ball, ie. your thought, under the water (classical CBT) and when you should just let it be

(Anti-CBT). The best answer I have come up with is that you need to judge whether the thought you are trying to manage is just a minor nuisance, and a little concerted logical effort can make it history, or the thought is so overwhelmingly big, that it makes all reasonable counter arguments seem irrelevant. So both methods, although on the surface contradictory, can work together as a united system.

There are many other modalities and approaches aimed at promoting emotional health. From food supplements to hypnotherapy and everything in between. I will avoid making a fool of myself by attempting to evaluate them or pass judgement. After all, the approaches are this diverse to express the diverse and varied needs of our friends and colleagues.

What I will say is that maintaining emotional health should be viewed the same way we advance other professional skills in our Veterinary life. It must be seen as an active process requiring effort, allocating time, open-minded research and a willingness to try and evaluate different approaches.

The Chapter With Nothing After It Yet

And so we come to the end of what I have to say. I should have really called this chapter 'Epilogue' or 'Conclusion' or the like. But I am not going to do that, because if this book is what I think it is - a brief summary of some of the many ideas I have about my work, then it shouldn't really have an ending. Every day we spend at work, we are learning to do our work better. Every day is an opportunity to improve. I hope that in the years to come this book will gain a few new chapters, just like you own mental manual of Veterinary solutions and tricks will gain a few pages of its' own. I hope there are things you have read here which you like and which you will find useful. There will undoubtedly be other things you don't like or feel you could do better. For all corrections, suggestions and scathing criticism, I have allocated a contact and will take them on board to the best of my ability. I am also (without claiming any particular skill in this area) offering to be a sounding board for those Veterinarians who are struggling professionally or emotionally.

The best way to contact me is through my blog at:

www.drvadim.org

I look forward to our future exchange of ideas.

Farewell and good luck.

Dr Vadim

www.ingramcontent.com/pod-product-compliance
Lightning Source LLC
Chambersburg PA
CBHW050056230526
45470CB00004B/1553